SUNDAY FUN DAY

AN ACTIVITY FOR EVERY WEEKEND OF THE YEAR

For Grace and Rose, who make every day a funday,
and in loving memory of my aunt Dotty
KH

For Eva, Iván, Olov, Jorun, and Nana
JV

First US edition 2022

First published by Nosy Crow Ltd (UK) 2021

Library of Congress Catalog Card Number 2021953325
ISBN 978-1-5362-2748-2

22 23 24 25 26 27 WKT 10 9 8 7 6 5 4 3 2 1

Printed in Shenzhen, Guangdong, China

This book was typeset in Futura.
The illustrations were created digitally.

Nosy Crow
an imprint of
Candlewick Press
99 Dover Street
Somerville, Massachusetts 02144

www.nosycrow.com
www.candlewick.com

Katherine Halligan

illustrated by

Jesús Verona

SUNDAY FUN DAY

AN ACTIVITY FOR EVERY
WEEKEND OF THE YEAR

nosy
crow

An imprint of Candlewick Press

CONTENTS

Introduction   6–7

SPRING

Natural Artist   10–11
Spring Snapshot   12–13
Springtime Shellebration   14–15
Be a Tree   16–17
Cool Carrot Cake   18–19
Radiant Raspberries   20
Top 10 Plants for Young Gardeners   21
Marvelous Minigarden   22
Noisy Nature Concert   23
Magic Beans   24–25
Sow a Minimeadow   26
Daisy, Daisy   27
Easy Peasy Cheesy Pasta   28
Secret Garden   29

SUMMER

Smile, It's a Smoothie   32
Fantastic Fruit Kebabs   33
Planting Pumpkins   34–35
Inspect an Insect   36–37
Small Space, Big Fun   38–39
Spectacular Sandcastles   40–41
Fantastic Nature Frame   42–43
Delicious Quiche   44–45
Adopt a Pet Rock   46
Wild Woodland Crown   47
Buoyant Leaf Boats   48
Press to Impress   49
Beautiful Butterfly Party   50–51

FALL

Fairy Homes	54–55
Soothing Soup	56–57
Leaf Lullaby Mobile	58–59
Outdoor Obstacle Course	60–61
Super Flower Surprise	62
Backyard Compost	63
Happy Apple Crumble	64–65
Nature Memory Jar	66–67
Tasty Granola	68–69
Carve a Spooky Pumpkin	70–71
Crispy Cinnamon Stars	72
Chalk Designs	73
Fantastic Bird Feast	74–75

WINTER

Shining Stars	78–79
Fabulous Fruity Wrapping Paper	80–81
Crafty Holiday Cookies	82–83
Present in a Pot	84
Winter Wildlife Tree	85
Perfect Pomanders	86
Cheerful Tree Sweater	87
Plant a Tree	88–89
Cozy Chicken Pie	90–91
Terrific Terrariums	92–93
Make a Pine Cone Pal	94–95
Gooey Grilled Cheese	96–97
Picture Treasure Hunt	98–99

Tools and Materials	100–101
Safety Tips	102
Index	103–104

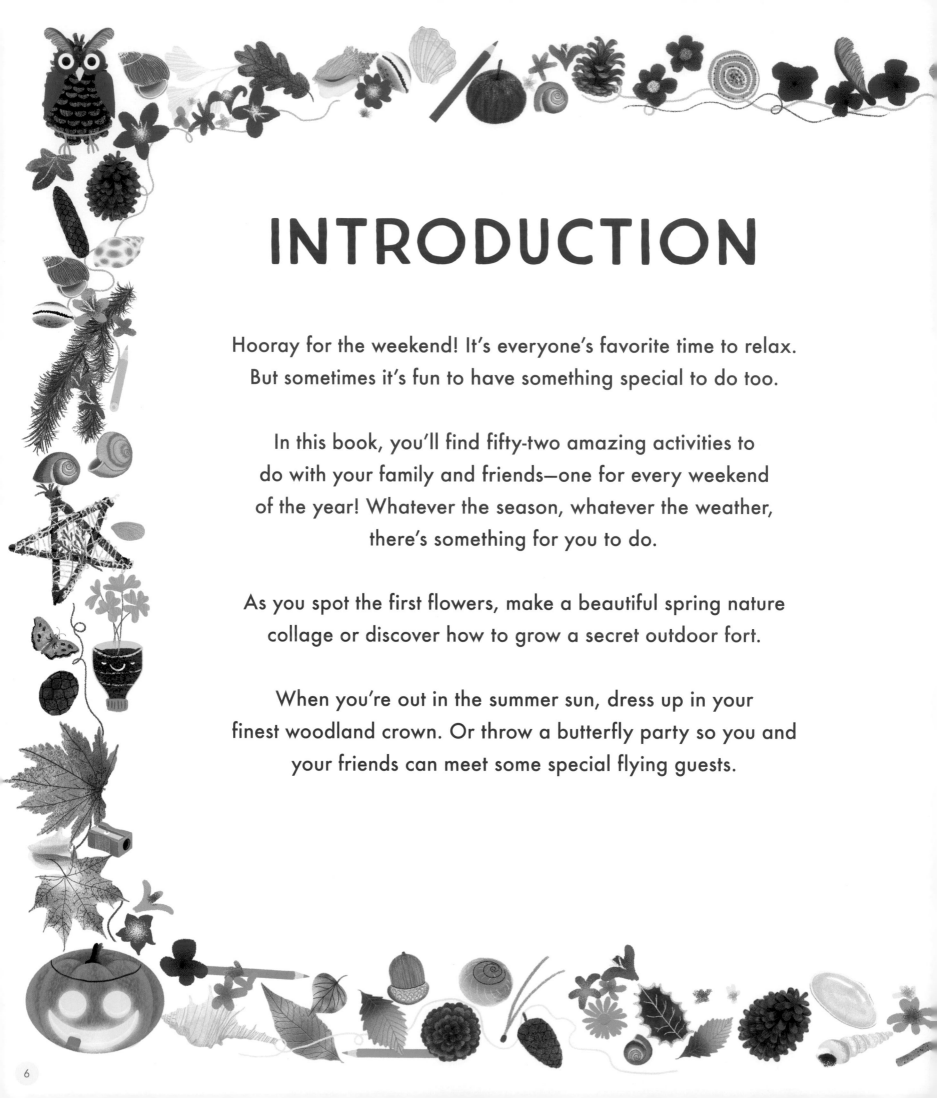

INTRODUCTION

Hooray for the weekend! It's everyone's favorite time to relax. But sometimes it's fun to have something special to do too.

In this book, you'll find fifty-two amazing activities to do with your family and friends—one for every weekend of the year! Whatever the season, whatever the weather, there's something for you to do.

As you spot the first flowers, make a beautiful spring nature collage or discover how to grow a secret outdoor fort.

When you're out in the summer sun, dress up in your finest woodland crown. Or throw a butterfly party so you and your friends can meet some special flying guests.

As the leaves turn colors and the days get colder in
fall, keep everyone warm with a scrumptious apple crumble,
then make a delicious feast for the birds outside.

The cold weather doesn't have to keep you inside.
When winter comes, brighten up the bare branches of
a tree with a cheerful cozy or even plant a tree of your very
own, then come home to play with a fantastic pine cone friend.

Before you get started, check out the Tools and Materials
lists at the back of the book for some helpful tips on what
you might need. Some of the activities in this book require
a grown-up's help, so make sure to have fun and be safe.

Whether you're out and about or staying snug and warm
inside, all these activities are perfect for you to have fun with
your family and friends. So make the weekend
the best part of your week, all year long!

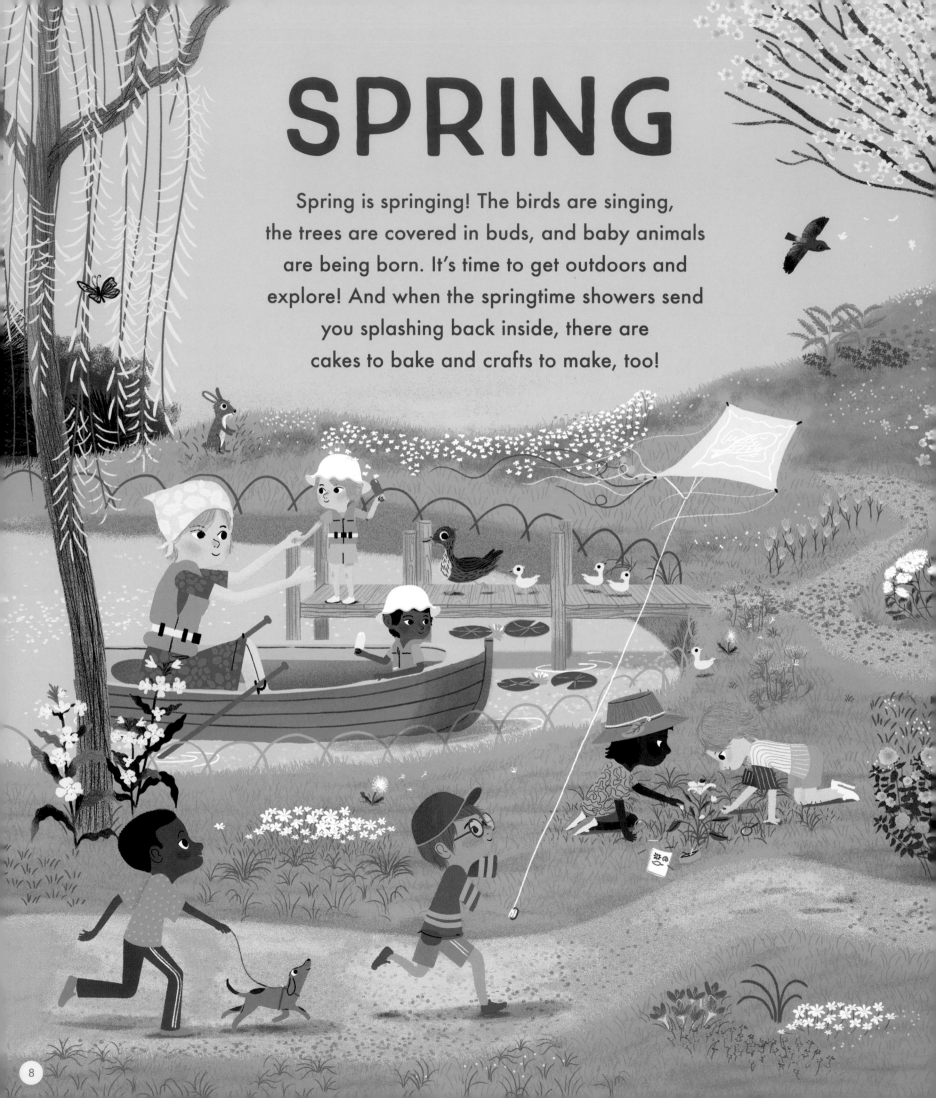

SPRING

Spring is springing! The birds are singing, the trees are covered in buds, and baby animals are being born. It's time to get outdoors and explore! And when the springtime showers send you splashing back inside, there are cakes to bake and crafts to make, too!

NATURAL ARTIST

You don't need fancy paintbrushes to make great art. Use twigs and leaves to create paintings and rubbings, just like some of the very first artists did!

TWIG-AND-LEAF PAINTING

Pick a nature paintbrush—or five! You can paint with just about anything. Use something with a "handle," like a twig or a flower on a stem. Or choose flatter items like stones to gently stamp paint onto the paper.

Once you've chosen your paintbrush, have some paint ready and a large, blank piece of craft paper. Now paint your picture!

Instead of thinking too much about what you are painting, notice how it feels when you paint. Think about the different marks each tool can make. What makes a thick line? What makes a brushy mark? Which is the hardest to paint with? Which is the most fun?

Try painting outdoors so you can have natural inspiration all around you while you work!

YOU WILL NEED:

natural paintbrushes: branches with leaves, twigs, seedpods, flowers, ferns, leaves of different shapes and sizes, or feathers

large sheet of craft paper

acrylic paint

paper towels

two pieces of white paper

crayons with the paper peeled off (wide crayons work best!)

LEAF RUBBING

Collect some leaves of all different shapes and sizes. If they feel wet, press them gently with a paper towel to make sure they are dry. Put one piece of white paper on a smooth, dry surface and place your leaves on the paper. Try arranging the leaves in a pattern or make a picture with them.

Now lay a second piece of white paper over the leaves. Use a crayon to rub firmly but gently across the top piece of paper, pressing down over the leaves to make a lovely, leafy print. Isn't it amazing how many different kinds of leaves there are?

SPRING SNAPSHOT

Create your own special snapshot of spring with a beautiful collage, using fantastic nature finds from your outdoor adventures.

Before you start, think about what you want to make. Do you want to glue your nature finds all over the paper in a random mix, or do you want to create a picture? For a picture, first try painting a background on the paper. When the paint is dry, you can glue your nature finds into place.

To protect your finished collage, mix a tablespoon of glue with a tablespoon of water. Using a soft, clean paintbrush, dab the watery glue all over the top of your finished picture and let it dry.

If you still have some leaves or pretty shells left over, make another one. No two pictures are ever the same!

YOU WILL NEED:

nature finds: shells, flowers, leaves, twigs

card stock or cardboard

glue

a paintbrush

paint (optional)

SPRINGTIME SHELLEBRATION

Pretty painted eggs are the perfect way to celebrate the arrival of spring. And if you blow your eggs before you decorate them, your creations will last for years to come!

Twist a pin carefully into the pointy end of the egg, twirling it back and forth until you break through the shell. If needed, ask a grown-up to make your hole a bit bigger by gently chipping away around the edges until it's about a millimeter wide.

Now make a hole in the other, wider end of the egg in the same way: it should be about twice the size of the first hole. Stick a paper clip or toothpick into the larger hole and wiggle it gently around to scramble up the inside of the egg.

Holding your egg over a bowl, gently blow into the smaller hole until the inside of the egg comes out of the bigger hole. If it doesn't come out easily, don't blow harder or your egg will crack! Just pop the paper clip or toothpick back in and wiggle it some more before blowing again. You and your grown-up can also try making both holes a bit bigger.

Clean your bowl, then add vinegar with cold water and use it to rinse out your egg. Then blow your egg again, until all the vinegar mixture has come out.

Leave your eggs out overnight so that they can dry.

Now it's time to decorate! You can use acrylic paint to make amazing designs or funny faces on your eggs, paint them in glue and dip them in glitter to make them sparkle, or even grab some dye and try out the patterns on the next page.

TO BLOW AN EGG, YOU WILL NEED:

an apron, since this can get messy!

eggs, at room temperature

a straight pin

a toothpick or paper clip

a bowl

a splash of white vinegar

acrylic paint

glue

glitter

TO DYE EGGS,
YOU WILL NEED:

blown or hard-boiled eggs (hard-boiled is easiest for younger children!)

crayons (white makes especially pretty designs, but any color that is different from your dye will work) or gold or silver permanent markers

a bowl

dye (either natural or from a packet; you can also use food coloring)

Use a crayon or marker to draw a design on your egg. It can be a picture or a pattern.

Dip the egg in a bowl with dye. If you are using a blown egg, hold it down with a spoon to keep it from floating up. The longer you leave your egg in the dye, the darker the color will be.

When you're ready, gently remove the egg from the dye and place it on some paper towel to dry.

BE A TREE

Did you know that a lot of yoga poses are named after plants and animals? Yoga is a great way to stretch and move your body—and these poses are even more fun to do outdoors! Try breathing slowly and deeply as you make these shapes with your body.

DOWNWARD-FACING DOG

TREE

Stand up tall. Pick a spot in front of you to look at. Keep your eyes on it to help keep your balance.

Start by lifting your left foot and placing it flat against your inner thigh or lower calf, with your left knee bent out to the side. Be careful not to place your foot against your knee. Bring your hands to your heart, palms together and fingers pointing straight up.

For an added challenge, try stretching your arms straight over your head. You can keep your palms together or move your arms out a bit wider, like the branches of a tree.

Now repeat on the other leg. Is one leg steadier? How long can you stay standing?

Stand up tall and reach your hands up to the sky.

Bend forward to put your hands on the ground on either side of your feet. Be sure to bend your knees as much as you need to.

Step both feet back so your bottom is up in the air. Straighten your arms and keep your legs slightly bent until you're comfortable straightening them as well. With your head hanging down, keep your neck relaxed. Be careful not to lift your head or look around because this can hurt your neck.

Imagine there is a rope around your hips pulling them back and up—so your back stays straight and long—and feel a lovely stretch in your back and legs!

YOU WILL NEED:

comfortable, stretchy clothes

a flat, open space

a yoga mat or a towel (optional)

CAT AND COW

Get down on all fours, keeping your back flat like a table and your eyes on the ground.

As you breathe in, lift your head to look forward (but don't tilt your head too far back) and arch your back so your tummy curves down toward the ground. This is called cow pose—moo!

As you breathe out, round your back and pull your belly button in toward your spine, with your arms straight and your head hanging down. This is called cat pose—meow! Follow your breath and repeat!

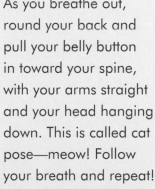

17

COOL CARROT CAKE

TOTAL

1 hour, 45 minutes

Makes 6–8 servings

A cake made of carrots? What could be a better springtime treat? And the delicious cream cheese frosting means the Easter bunny won't be the only one who will love it!

Ask a grown-up to preheat the oven to 325°F (170°C). You will need to prep two round cake pans that are the same size, about 8 inches (20 centimeters) across. Grease your pans with butter, and then line the bottom with baking parchment.

In a bowl, beat together the sugar, oil, eggs, flour, baking soda, salt, ground cinnamon, and vanilla extract until it forms a smooth mixture.

Next, stir in the grated carrots, using a wooden spoon. Mix well before spooning the cake mixture evenly into your two prepared cake pans.

Bake in the oven for 40–45 minutes. To tell if your cake is done, a grown-up should stick a toothpick into the middle; if it comes out clean, your cake is ready! Ask a grown-up to turn out the cakes onto a wire cooling rack and remove the baking parchment. Let the cake cool completely before you frost it.

FOR THE CAKE, YOU WILL NEED:

butter (to grease the pans)

2 cups sugar

1¼ cups sunflower oil

4 eggs

2¼ cups plain flour

2 teaspoons baking soda

1 teaspoon salt

1 teaspoon ground cinnamon

1 teaspoon vanilla extract

3 cups grated carrots

FOR THE FROSTING, YOU WILL NEED:

½ cup unsalted butter, softened

2 teaspoons vanilla extract

8 ounces cream cheese

2 cups sifted powdered sugar

orange and green food coloring

a piping bag

It's a good idea to make the frosting while the cake bakes. Mix the softened butter until it is creamy and light. Add the vanilla extract, then slowly add in the cream cheese and the sifted powdered sugar, mixing the entire time until there are no lumps.

Set aside two spoonfuls of frosting in two small bowls. Use a third of the remaining frosting to sandwich the two cake layers together. Then spread the rest of the frosting over the cake until it's covered.

In the first small bowl, squeeze in four drops of orange food coloring and mix. In the second small bowl, add four drops of green food coloring and mix well.

Finally, put the orange frosting into a piping bag and ask a grown-up to help you squeeze out carrot shapes to decorate the cake. If you don't have a piping bag, use a plastic sandwich bag with a corner cut off to decorate your cake. Once all the carrots are drawn, wash out the piping bag, then add the green frosting to make leaves. Now it's time to eat!

RADIANT RASPBERRIES

Raspberries are easy to grow. They look beautiful and taste delicious! Growing raspberries from seed takes a few months, but it's worth the wait.

Ask a grown-up to help you prepare empty yogurt cups by making small holes in the bottom for drainage. Then fill them with special seed-starting soil.

Take a handful of raspberries and mash them up with the back of a wooden spoon in a sieve. Pick the brown seeds out of the red pulp and set them aside. Then you can eat the juicy pulp on its own or with yogurt—yum!

Plant the seeds about 1 inch (2 centimeters) apart and ½ inch (1 centimeter) deep. Spray them with water, but remember that they don't like to get too wet.

After around 4–6 weeks, you will see your first baby raspberry plants! When your seedlings are around 1 inch (2 centimeters) tall and it's at least 60°F (15°C) outside, plant them in the ground or in a big pot. As they grow, tie them to bamboo canes. After the plants have flowered, watch for the first little berries to appear!

YOU WILL NEED:

empty yogurt cups

seed-starting soil

raspberries

a wooden spoon

a sieve

a spray bottle of water

bamboo canes

TOP 10 PLANTS FOR YOUNG GARDENERS

peas

tomatoes

strawberries

radishes

carrots

lettuces

pumpkins

hollyhocks

nasturtiums

sunflowers

MARVELOUS MINIGARDEN

Most gardens are big, but some gardens are tiny and can even be grown indoors. Make a garden for your favorite tiny toys.

First, decorate a pot or tray however you like. When it's ready, put the pot on a plate. Scoop in soil until the pot is three-quarters full.

Scatter grass seed over the top, spray with water, and wait for the magic to happen!

Once the grass begins to grow, think about what you want to add to your garden. You could use toy furniture or make your own out of paper and cardboard.

Now add a bit of fun with different toys and stuffed animals!

YOU WILL NEED:

a small pot or tray with holes in the bottom

things to decorate your pot such as stickers, paper, fabric, paint, ribbons, or sequins

potting soil

a handful of grass seeds

a spray bottle of water

small toys, fairies, dragons . . . whatever you like!

things for making furniture, such as cardboard, glue, scissors, etc.

NOISY NATURE CONCERT

Nature is full of so many different noises, more than enough to put together a nature concert! You can use anything to make music outdoors, but here are a few ideas to help get you started.

YOU WILL NEED:

empty bottles

tiny pebbles

tape

a few glasses

two straight, strong twigs per person

rocks or stones

Fill bottles with tiny pebbles. Fasten the lids very tightly and tape them down, then shake the bottles like maracas!

Ask a grown-up to help you fill a few glasses with different amounts of water. Tap a twig very gently on the sides of each glass to hear the different sounds. Can you play a tune?

Use strong twigs like drumsticks to beat out rhythms on logs, rocks, walls, or paving stones. Listen to the different sounds and decide which you like best.

Hold a stone in each hand and tap them together. What kind of sounds do you hear when you use different sizes and types of stones?

MAGIC BEANS

Every seed has a whole plant inside it, just waiting to sprout. Planting seeds is great fun, and it's magical watching those first shoots uncurl!

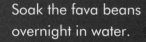

Soak the fava beans overnight in water.

Scrunch the paper towel or cotton balls down into a cup or jar.

Tuck the beans inside the paper towel or cotton balls. Spray them with water until they feel damp, then put the cup or jar on a sunny windowsill.

Check your baby beans every day. Keep the paper towel or cotton balls moist, but don't let water sit in the bottom of the jar.

After 1–2 weeks, the beans will sprout. Roots will start to push down, and leaves will start to pop up. Hooray, baby beans!

25

SOW A MINIMEADOW

Wildflowers are so pretty, and they provide food for bees, butterflies, and other wildlife too. You can sow seeds anywhere you find a little patch of soil in your yard! If you have a sunny spot, try planting flowers like daisies, black-eyed Susans, purple coneflowers, poppies, or cornflowers. In shadier areas, try primroses and bluebells.

Get a patch of ground ready by removing any stones or roots and raking the soil until it's nice and crumbly and flat.

Next, mix the seeds with sand so you can see where they are. Then sprinkle them all over your patch of soil. Be careful not to drop them all in one spot though, or they won't have room to grow.

Now rake the soil to cover the seeds. Keep watering them well until green shoots start to poke out of the ground. Your minimeadow will soon be filled with color!

YOU WILL NEED:

a small shovel

a rake

packets of wildflower seeds

sand

a small trowel

a watering can

DAISY, DAISY

lots of daisies—about 5 for a bracelet and 10–12 for a necklace or crown

a quiet place to sit

There's nothing as delightful as a daisy chain! Make pretty spring necklaces and bracelets for you and all your friends.

First, pick some daisies.
Make sure they have nice, long stems, but be careful not to pull up the roots of the plant.

Choose your first daisy. Use your thumbnail to make a small slit near the bottom of the stem.

Poke the stem of your second daisy through the hole you have created, gently pulling it all the way through. This is the start of your chain.

Now make a slit in the stem of the second daisy and pull your third daisy stem through. Repeat until you have made your chain as long as you like.

To finish your chain, make a bigger slit in the last stem and carefully slip the flower head of the first daisy through to fasten it. Then put it on, or give it to a friend!

EASY PEASY CHEESY PASTA

15 minutes

Makes 2–4 servings

After a busy day, it's always nice to relax over a tasty dinner with family and friends. And dinnertime is even more enjoyable when you're sharing something you've made yourself!

YOU WILL NEED:

2 cups dried pasta (any shape is fine!)

⅓ cup fresh or frozen peas

3 tablespoons grated hard cheese (or more, if you like!)

2 teaspoons unsalted butter and/or 1 tablespoon olive oil

2 tablespoons of ricotta or heavy cream

salt and pepper to taste

Ask a grown-up to help you bring a large pot of water to a boil and add the pasta. Cook it for as long as advised on the package—usually 10–12 minutes. If you are using frozen peas, add them to the pot about one minute before your pasta is finished cooking.

When the pasta has finished cooking, ask a grown-up to drain the water using a colander and pour the pasta back into the pot. If you are using fresh peas, add them to the drained pasta and stir well to steam them. Then add the grated cheese, butter or oil, ricotta or heavy cream, and salt and pepper, and stir it again. Your easy peasy cheesy pasta is now ready to serve!

Yummy!

SECRET GARDEN

Have you ever wanted your own secret hideout?
Then try growing a garden fort! Who knows what awesome
adventures you will have in your living garden playhouse?

Decide on the place where you want to put your fort. Ask a grown-up to help you dig
and weed a circle of soil, then rake it until it's nice and crumbly. Leave a gap on one
side of the circle. Stick the bamboo canes firmly into the ground around the circle,
then have a grown-up help tie them together at the top into a cone shape.

Now water the soil so it's wet but not too muddy, and sow the seeds around
the circle, close to each cane. Make sure to choose plants that grow tall or have
lots of vines. Remember not to plant seeds in the space left
as an entrance. As the vines start to grow, gently tie them
to the canes using gardening string.

After two months, the canes will be covered with
vines, and you will have a secret hideout inside!

YOU WILL NEED:

a shovel, a rake, and a hoe

5 or 6 equally tall, strong bamboo canes

a watering can

**vine seeds: sweet peas, runner beans,
climbing nasturtium, morning glories,
peas, or honeysuckle**

6–10 feet (2–3 meters) of gardening string

SUMMER

Here come the lazy, hazy days of summer! It's the perfect time to get outside and play in the yard. It's also a wonderful time to walk in the woods or play at the beach, so here are lots of ideas to make your weekends extra special!

TOTAL

15 minutes

Makes 4–6 smoothies

SMILE, IT'S A SMOOTHIE

Smoothies are quick and delicious. Full of fruity goodness and packed with protein and calcium from milk and yogurt, they give you everything you need to get ready for the day!

Ask a grown-up to help you peel and chop the fruit. Then pop it all into a blender. Make sure to keep the blender unplugged until you're ready to mix. Then, add the yogurt and milk. If you are using bananas, they will make your smoothie thicker, so add a little more milk. If you are using fresh fruit, you might also want to add some ice cubes to keep your smoothie cold.

Now put the lid firmly on the blender and ask your grown-up to plug it in. Press the button and watch it whirl.

Before you pour out your smoothie, ask a grown-up to unplug the blender. Then try a spoonful—if it's not sweet enough, add some honey and start the blender again. Repeat as necessary until your smoothie is just how you like it.

Pour into cups and enjoy!

YOU WILL NEED:

2 cups fresh or frozen fruit: apricots, peaches, kiwis, bananas, blueberries, strawberries, and maybe even the radiant raspberries you've grown in your garden; remember, softer fruit makes a smoother smoothie!

1 cup plain yogurt

½ cup milk

ice cubes (optional)

2 teaspoons honey (optional)

FANTASTIC FRUIT KEBABS

This is fruit salad on a stick! It's so much fun to eat, especially at a picnic!

TOTAL

15 minutes
Makes as many as you like!

Ask a grown-up to help you chop all the fruit into 1-inch (2–3-centimeter) chunks. You can cut soft fruit with a table knife.

Pierce the fruit with the skewers. Be careful of the sharp end of the skewer. You may need a grown-up to help you get started so you don't poke your hand.

See how many great patterns you can make with all the different colored fruit. If you are using coconut too, sprinkle it on a plate and roll the skewers in the flakes.

Before you share the fruit kebabs with friends, ask a grown-up to cut off the sharp end of the skewers. This will make them safe and fun to eat!

YOU WILL NEED:

pineapple

strawberries

orange

mango

peaches or nectarines (pits removed)

kiwi (white center removed)

melon (cantaloupe, honeydew, watermelon—or all three!)

grapes (for children under six, grapes should be cut in half vertically)

wooden skewers

½ cup shredded coconut (optional)

PLANTING PUMPKINS

Plump pumpkins are fun to grow and fun to eat—the perfect fall treat! But they need to soak up the sun all summer long, so now is the time to prepare your perfect pumpkin patch!

Pumpkins love space and sunlight! The best time to plant is early to mid-June, as your pumpkins will need at least three months of warm summer weather to grow. If you don't have a big space, you can grow smaller types of pumpkin or use big containers or pots instead. Make sure the pots have plenty of holes in the bottom to let water drain out.

Pumpkins also like rich soil, so add lots of manure and compost (see page 63) and mix it all together.

Now it's time to plant your seeds. Make a row of little hills, around 32 inches (80 centimeters) wide each and 3–6 feet (1–2 meters) apart.

Plant 2–3 seeds in every hill, about 1 inch (2 centimeters) deep. Water them well.

In less than a week, you will see the first shoots poking out. These should grow into little pumpkin seedlings in 5–10 days. Hooray!

When the pumpkin plants grow flowers, they need the help of bees. Bees carry pollen from flower to flower, which is what makes the flowers grow pumpkins. If you use fertilizer, try not to use one with chemicals that will hurt insects.

YOU WILL NEED:

pumpkin seeds

a large sunny patch of soil, or 8–gallon (30–liter) containers

compost and manure

a shovel

fertilizer

a watering can

You can also grow other plants and flowers that will attract bees (see pages 50–51).

After the flowers have bloomed, the plants will start to grow tiny pumpkins.

Look after your pumpkins as they grow. If they are lying on their side, turn them very gently every so often to help them grow in an even shape. You can also slide a piece of cardboard underneath them to keep them from rotting or getting eaten by hungry bugs.

Your pumpkins are ready to pick when they are bright orange and the outer skin (called a rind) is hard. If you press your fingernail into the pumpkin, the rind should be strong enough for your nail not to break it.

INSPECT AN INSECT

Insects are amazing. Sometimes we call them bugs or pests, but did you know that many insects can be very useful in the garden? Bees carry pollen from flower to flower, which helps plants make new seeds. Ladybugs eat the aphids that eat plants. Which garden creatures can you find? Just remember—look but don't touch!

butterfly

leatherjacket

aphids

lacewing

ground beetle

spider

snail

Go out into your yard, local park, or nature area. Look for insects by moving slowly and quietly. You will usually find them on or under plants. Sometimes they are down in the grass.

Use your magnifying glass to get a closer look. Can you guess which kind of insect you are looking at? If you're not sure, draw a picture of the interesting insect and then look it up when you get home.

dragonfly

leafhoppers

YOU WILL NEED:

a pencil

a small notebook
or piece of paper

a magnifying glass

bumblebee

ladybug

weevil

butterfly

crane fly

earwig

honeybee

spider

caterpillar

wood lice

earthworm

37

SMALL SPACE, BIG FUN!

Even if you don't have a yard, there are still plenty of ways
to get growing. From window boxes to old rubber boots,
you can grow plants almost anywhere!

WINDOW BOX WOW

Ask a grown-up to add some holes to the bottom of a window box to let water drain out. Cover the holes with garden mesh and attach the box to a wall or windowsill. Then fill the box with soil and get planting!

YOU WILL NEED:

a window box

garden mesh

potting soil

plants

old rubber boots, any size

small nails

a hammer

cracked teapots or extra cups

an old hat

a plastic bag

GROWING SHOOTS IN RUBBER BOOTS

If you have some old rubber boots, don't throw them away. Turn them into plant pots instead! Ask a grown-up to help you poke holes in the soles of the boots by tapping a nail through with a hammer. Then fill with soil and your favorite plants.

TEA PARTY GARDEN

Make a tea party garden by filling cracked teapots or cups with soil and plants! Old sun hats make great hanging gardens too. Fill an old plastic bag with soil and a plant, tie the bag in a loose knot around the stem, and then poke small holes in the bag. Now make a hole in the side of your hat and lift the plant leaves through, keeping the bag inside the hat. Finally, ask a grown-up to hang your plant hat from a wall.

PLANT POTS FOR THE PLANET

The best way to help the planet is to reduce, reuse, and recycle, so why not get creative and use other old objects in your home for plant pots too? From sinks to sandboxes and cans to colanders, plants will grow happily in just about anything! As long as they have drainage holes and good soil, everything from recycled bottles to muffin pans can be made into a new home for a plant!

SPECTACULAR SANDCASTLES

Building sandcastles is one of the best summer activities ever! But if you can't get to the beach, you can make one in a sandpit in your local playground or at home.

If you are at the beach, pick a spot that's close to the water but far enough away to keep you and your castle safe from surprise waves!

Make sure the sand is nice and wet. It's best when the sand is soaked but not slushy.

Dig a moat around the space for your castle and fill it with water.

Build up the walls of your castle by scooping and packing sand into the shape you want.

To build towers, pack your bucket firmly with sand, right up to the top and a bit over—if you leave empty space, your tower will crack and crumble.

YOU WILL NEED:

plenty of sand

some water

a small shovel (but hands make great scoopers, too!)

a small bucket

seashells, seaweed, or toys for decoration

Keep one hand on top of the sand until the very last minute, then turn your bucket over carefully and press it firmly into the ground.

Tap it gently on top, then s-l-o-o-o-o-w-l-y slide your bucket up off the packed sand and—voilà—a tower!

Add more towers and decorate with shells, seaweed, or even small toys, then stand back and admire your finished castle!

FANTASTIC NATURE FRAME

This makes a great gift for any occasion. Just pop in a picture—either a photo or a drawing—and wrap it up for someone special!

YOU WILL NEED:

scissors

2 small pieces of card stock or cardboard

4 craft sticks

glue

markers

paint and a paintbrush

nature finds like small seashells, leaves, or twigs

Ask a grown-up to help you cut out a square of card stock so that each side is about 1 inch (3 centimeters) shorter than your craft sticks.

Glue down two craft sticks, one along the top and one along the bottom edge of the cut card stock, so that the sticks poke out over the edges of the card stock by about ½ inch (1.5 centimeters) on each side. Put a dot of glue on each end of the craft sticks where they line up with the corners of the card stock.

Lay a craft stick along the left and right sides of the square over the glue dots, again with about ½ inch (1.5 centimeters) poking out over each corner of the card stock. This is your frame. Press the corners down firmly and set aside to dry.

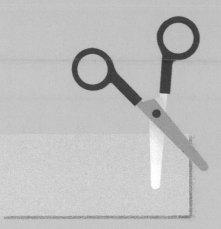

Cut a second piece of card stock into a narrow rectangle that is 1½–2 inches (5 centimeters) wide and about 1 inch (2 centimeters) longer than the square.

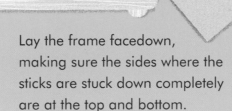

Lay the frame facedown, making sure the sides where the sticks are stuck down completely are at the top and bottom.

Fold back the top 1 inch (2 centimeters) of the rectangular card stock. Center and glue the folded part of the rectangle to the top of the frame.

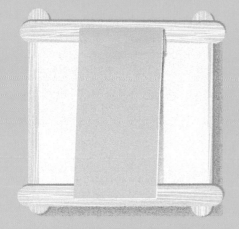

The bottom edge of the rectangle should line up with the bottom of the frame. Leave it facedown until it's dry.

Now it's time to decorate the frame. Color it with paint or markers, or glue shells, twigs, and other nature finds around the edges, and then leave it to dry.

Choose a photo or drawing. You may have to trim it so it's just a bit smaller than the opening in your frame. Slide it in from the side, where the craft sticks don't lie flat against the card stock. What a perfect picture!

DELICIOUS QUICHE

Quiche tastes delicious hot or cold, and it makes the perfect packed lunch for any outdoor adventure! You can try lots of different fillings, but here are a few ideas to get you started.

FOR THE PASTRY, YOU WILL NEED:

2½ cups flour

1 teaspoon salt

1 cup unsalted butter

5–6 tablespoons cold water

Mix the flour and salt in a bowl. Cut the butter into small cubes, and add to the mix. With your fingers, combine the flour and butter together until it looks like fine breadcrumbs. Then slowly add the water, a little at a time. Keep adding water until you can shape the pastry into a ball. Wrap the ball in a wax wrap or aluminum foil and chill it in the fridge for at least 15 minutes before rolling it out.

TOTAL

1 hour, or 1 hour 20 minutes (if making pastry)

Makes 6–8 servings

Ask a grown-up to preheat the oven to 350°F (180°C).

Grease an 8-inch (20-centimeter) quiche or pie pan, or for miniquiches, a 12-cup muffin pan.

Roll your pastry out with a well-floured rolling pin, then lay it in the pan, gently pressing it into the corners.

Use a butter knife to remove extra pastry. For miniquiches, use an upside-down mug or a pastry cutter to cut your pastry bases, and gently press them into your muffin pan. Prick the pastry base with a fork.

FOR THE QUICHE, YOU WILL NEED:

shortcrust pastry (see above for recipe) or a 14-ounce premade pastry shell

1½ cups grated cheddar cheese

6 eggs

1 cup chopped spinach, diced ham, cooked bacon, chopped onions, broccoli, apples—whatever you like!

¾ cup milk

¼ cup heavy cream

Spread the grated cheese onto the pan lined with the pastry base. In a bowl, beat the eggs. Add the milk, heavy cream, and other fillings to the bowl, then pour the eggy mixture into the pan.

Bake for 35–40 minutes for a large quiche or 15–20 minutes for miniquiches, until golden on top and firm.

You can ask a grown-up to test if the quiche is cooked by sticking a knife gently into the center; if it comes out clean, it's ready.

45

ADOPT A PET ROCK

These painted rocks make perfect
presents or friends to play with.
Why not make a whole family
of pets with funny faces?

Find a rock you like.
Make sure it's clean
and dry. Now paint
your rock into a pet,
or a person, or
whatever you like!

Be creative in your design! If you
have googly eyes, you can glue
these on once the paint is dry.
Maybe add feathers for hair, or
try ears made of pom-poms to
bring your new friend to life!

YOU WILL NEED:

a smooth rock—about
the size of your palm

a small paintbrush

paint

fun decorations, such as
googly eyes, pom-poms,
feathers, or glitter

glue

WILD WOODLAND CROWN

Have you ever wanted to be nature royalty?
Well, this project is for you!

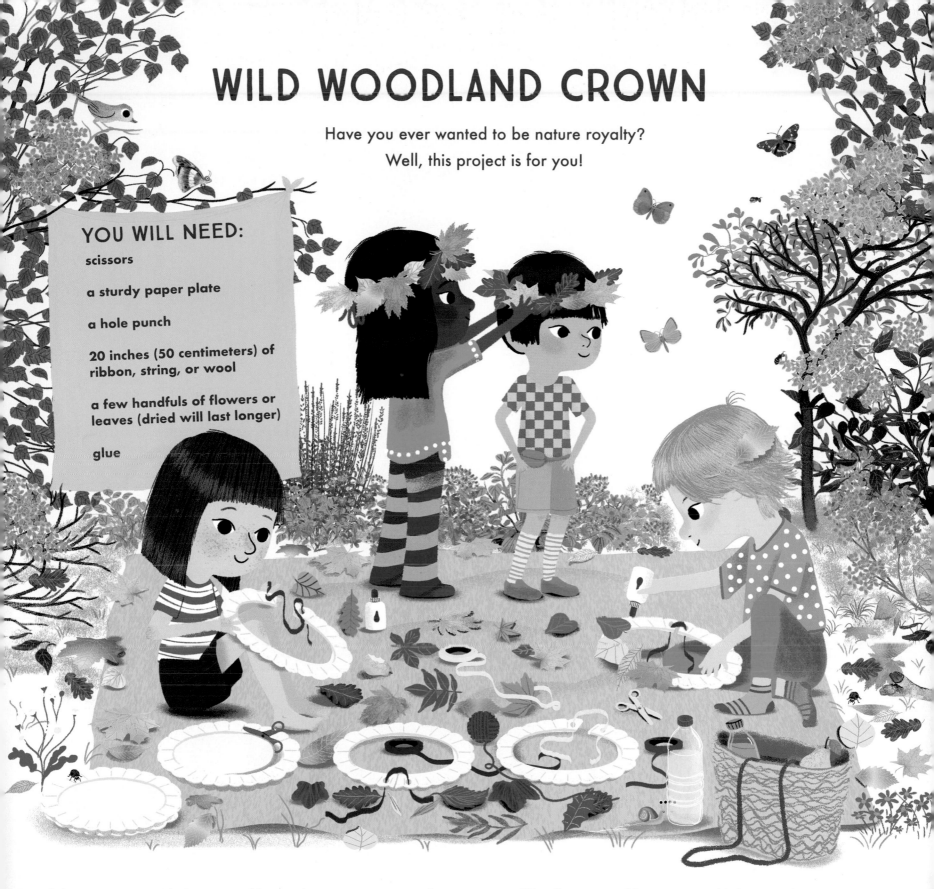

YOU WILL NEED:

scissors

a sturdy paper plate

a hole punch

20 inches (50 centimeters) of ribbon, string, or wool

a few handfuls of flowers or leaves (dried will last longer)

glue

Ask a grown-up to help you cut into a plate across the rim, then cut out a circle around the middle, leaving an edge of 1–1½ inches (3–4 centimeters).

Next, ask a grown-up to make a hole at each end of the plate, near the break in the rim. Thread a piece of string or ribbon through each hole and fasten it to the plate with a knot. This is how you will tie the crown to your head.

Glue flowers and leaves on the top side of the paper crown or outer edge of the band. You can use real nature decorations or make your own.

Make sure the crown is completely dry before you put it on, so it doesn't stick to your hair, and enjoy being crowned leader of the forest!

BUOYANT LEAF BOATS

You can set sail with just two leaves, a twig, and a little bit of water! Try making boats with different kinds of leaves to see which type works best.

Find two or three strong and slightly curved leaves, a bigger one for the boat and smaller ones for the sails. You could even use a curved piece of tree bark. For sails, the best leaves are light and thin.

Make a sail by poking a twig, now a mast, into the top part of the smaller leaf (about a third of the way down from the top), then push it down and make another hole (about a third of the way up from the bottom). Add a second sail if your twig is long enough to fit one.

Now stick the newly made mast and sail into the bigger, stronger leaf or a piece of bark. If the leaf is curved and the hole will sit just above the water, poke the mast just a little way through. If not, use mud to keep the mast and sail in place.

Wait until it's dry, then launch your boat on its voyage!

PRESS TO IMPRESS

Pressed flowers and leaves make beautiful gifts. You can frame them, stick them on homemade greeting cards, or turn them into bookmarks. Try dahlia petals in the fall, pansies in the winter, or violets in the spring.

YOU WILL NEED:

flowers such as daisies, delphinium, cosmos, or single-petal roses; always ask permission before picking!

leaves with interesting shapes, such as ferns, oak, or maple

newspaper, parchment paper, blotting paper, or card stock

some heavy books

It's best to pick flowers or leaves on a sunny morning, after the dew has evaporated. Make sure your finds are completely dry, then place them between two layers of dry paper or card stock, sandwiched between two heavy books.

Now lay even more books on top!

Leave for 7–10 days, then open up and, presto—pressed flowers and leaves!

49

BEAUTIFUL BUTTERFLY PARTY

Butterflies love bright colors. So if you want to see lots of butterflies, wear colorful clothes and have a special picnic near your new fluttery friends!

YOU WILL NEED:

brightly colored clothing, ideally with flowers on it

a picnic blanket

snacks for you and your human friends

a drawing pad

colored pencils or crayons

Dress like a butterfly in your most colorful clothes. At a park or garden, lay your blanket near the brightest flowers you can find! Butterflies especially love milkweed, goldenrod, and lilacs.

Sit quietly and enjoy watching the butterflies come to join in your picnic. If you hold very still, they might think you're a flower and land on you!

Draw all the butterflies you see, so you can look up their names later. How many did you see? Which flowers were they most attracted to? If you could be a butterfly, which one would you be?

BE KIND TO BEES, PLEASE!

Bees might seem a little scary because they can sting, but bees are a gardener's friend. They carry pollen from flower to flower, helping plants grow.

GIVE YOUR GARDEN WINGS

Bees, butterflies, and birds all help gardens grow and keep the world healthy and beautiful! Try planting some of the herbs and plants below to attract the flying visitors.

PRETTY PLANTS:

milkweed, sunflowers, purple coneflowers, marigolds, honeysuckle, sage, alyssum, evening primroses, lavender

HELPFUL HERBS:

rosemary, lemon balm, chives, dill, thyme, verbena, oregano, yarrow, mint, fennel, cilantro

FALL

The leaves are turning colors and starting to drop, pumpkins are growing plump, the days are getting shorter, and the nights are getting chilly. It must be fall! Here are a few ways to enjoy this golden time of year.

FAIRY HOMES

Every fairy needs a little home to call their own!
Fairies can live anywhere; all you need are a few pots and plants!
And if you don't have everything you need in your own yard,
try collecting items from your local park.

YOU WILL NEED:

fallen leaves, twigs and sticks, moss, stones, bark—anything you can find to build with!

flowers (make sure to ask before picking any)

seed fluff, from milkweed or dandelions

acorns

Find a secluded spot in your yard or start with a pot of grass or the marvelous minigarden you've already created.

Begin by building a structure. Try leaning lots of twigs up against a tree, using the tree trunk as one wall, or make a cone shape by leaning the tops of the twigs against one another and spreading the base out in a larger circle.

If you have soft ground, try pushing the ends of the twigs down into the soil using a stone for a hammer, but watch your fingers! Stick the twigs close together to make walls, and leave a gap for the door. Use pieces of flat bark or more twigs to make a roof. Maybe even line the roof with moss or leaves.

Or, if there aren't enough sticks, try stacking small stones on top of each other to build a house.

Now it's time to make some furniture. Flat stones make good tables. Ask a grown-up to saw a thick branch into small flat circles for tables and chairs. The best beds are made of leaves or soft moss. Large flower petals or some seed fluff make beautiful blankets.

Fairies need to eat too, and nature makes perfect bowls and cups for them! If you find acorns, pull off the little tops and turn them upside down. You can even pour a little water into them, in case the fairies are thirsty.

Once you're finished, include your pine cone creations (see pages 94–95) and let your local fairies discover their new home. Tiptoe back quietly the next morning— you may find that you've had some magical visitors in the night!

SOOTHING SOUP

Soup is a great way to warm up on a cold evening, or makes a light dinner in the summertime. This recipe involves a lot of chopping, so make sure to let a grown-up handle the knife, but everyone can help to measure, open, sort, and pour!

YOU WILL NEED:

1 tablespoon olive oil

2 pieces of bacon, chopped (optional)

½ an onion, chopped

3 cups carrots, chopped

1 clove garlic, crushed

4 cups chicken or vegetable stock

one 15-ounce can
of chopped tomatoes

½ teaspoon oregano

½ teaspoon thyme

salt and pepper to taste

¾ cup dried red lentils

1 cup peas, fresh or frozen

Ask a grown-up to heat oil in a large saucepan over medium heat, then gently fry the bacon, onions, and carrots for about 10 minutes until the vegetables are soft, stirring occasionally.

Add the garlic and fry for another minute. Make sure to keep stirring once the garlic has been added so it doesn't burn.

Pour in the stock, canned tomatoes, oregano, thyme, salt, and pepper. Bring to a boil, then turn down the heat, stir well, and cover. Simmer for 10 minutes.

Add the lentils and cook for another 15 minutes or until the lentils are completely soft. Then turn off the heat, add the peas, and stir.

Allow the soup to cool slightly. Ask a grown-up to ladle the soup into a blender, or to use an immersion blender to blend the soup in the pan. Blend until the soup is thick but not too lumpy. Warm the soup through again, stir well, and serve.

LEAF LULLABY MOBILE

Just because it's bedtime doesn't mean you have to say good night to nature!
Bring the magic of the outdoors inside with your own beautiful mobile.

Cut two pieces of string that are about 12 inches (30 centimeters) long.

Hold the two twigs firmly together in an X shape and wrap the first piece of string back and forth around the place where the twigs cross, over and over again until you have about 2 inches (5 centimeters) of loose string left free at each end.

Lay the second 12-inch (30-centimeter) piece of string across the place where the twigs intersect.

Tie the ends of the first piece of string with a double knot to tightly secure the second piece of string to the twigs.

Fold the second piece of string in half to make a loop for hanging your mobile, and tie those ends in another double knot.

Now cut five pieces of string into different lengths, 6–12 inches (15–30 centimeters) long. Tie one end of string to the middle of where the twigs intersect. Tie the other four pieces of string to the four twig ends.

Tie or glue your nature finds onto the ends of the dangling strings.

Hang your mobile in a window—or over the foot of your bed—and enjoy. Sweet dreams!

> ### SAFETY TIP:
> Never hang anything with strings near the head of your bed in case it falls down. Make sure dangling strings are always 12 inches (30 centimeters) or shorter in length.

YOU WILL NEED:

6–10 feet (2–3 meters) sturdy string

two sturdy, straight twigs, about the same length

nature finds like small pine cones, feathers, shells . . . or any other natural thing that catches your eye!

scissors and glue

YOU WILL NEED:

sturdy shoes

lots of fallen leaves or twigs

several large, flat stones

a log or large fallen branch

a watch or phone with a timer (if you want a friend to time how long it takes you to finish the course)

START

First, find a space for your adventure course: it should be open and flat, and not in the middle of a path. If it's near a very narrow stream for jumping across, even better! Then take a look around you, and start planning.

It's best to create your course around the logs, leaves, and rocks that are already there. If you do move a few items around, make sure to check that nothing is living on or under them.

OUTDOOR OBSTACLE COURSE

The woods have so many natural obstacles, so if you feel like hopping, jumping, and running, try making your very own nature adventure course!

A log or fallen branch can be a balance beam or an obstacle to jump over. Lay a branch across two large stones or stumps to crawl under, but first check for sharp rocks or sticks.

Line up a few stones with space in between them and leap from stone to stone.

Use leaves or twigs to create a couple of circles, close together: try to jump to each circle with both feet, or hop on one foot.

Once you have arranged your course, warm up by jogging in place, doing a few jumping jacks, and stretching. If you're using a timer, have it ready. Then go to the START line!

SUPER FLOWER SURPRISE

Bulbs might look plain and brown, but there is a beautiful flower inside, just waiting to pop up in the spring after a long winter's nap. Plant some now to enjoy them next spring, and then year after year!

YOU WILL NEED:

a flat, sunny spot in the garden or a large pot or other container that's around 8 gallons (30 liters) with plenty of drainage holes

a rake or a small gardening fork

potting soil (if planting in a container)

several bulbs, such as daffodils, crocuses, tulips, or hyacinths

compost

sand

a shovel

Plan to plant your bulbs about six weeks before the first frost. Store your bulbs in a paper bag in a cool, dry place until you are ready to plant.

Prepare the soil by removing any weeds and roots, then raking it so it is nice and crumbly. Bulbs need about six hours of sunlight a day, so make sure the spot is not too shady. You could also stir in a bit of compost and some sand to give your bulbs a happy home.

Dig a small hole about three times as deep as your bulb is tall. Then plant the bulbs with the stringy root at the bottom and the pointy part facing up. Cover them with soil and press down firmly so there are no air pockets, which can make the bulbs rot.

Fill your flower bed with bulbs, planting them 2–4 inches (6–10 centimeters) apart. Water them regularly, but don't let them get too soggy.

Then watch for those first green shoots in the spring, and see what surprises they bring!

BACKYARD COMPOST

Making compost is another way to have messy fun outside—and it's great for your garden, too.

First, you'll need to find a good compost bin. You could use a crate or ask a grown-up to nail together old fencing or wooden crates to make one.

Fill the compost bin with a layer of green things, such as grass cuttings, green leaves, and fruit and vegetable scraps. Water it well.

Now add a layer of brown things, such as dried leaves, pine needles, or even old newspapers, and water it again. Add some soil and—you guessed it, more water.

Cover the compost bin to keep the moisture and good bacteria inside. Every few weeks, use a shovel to mix the compost together.

When it looks dark and crumbly, it's ready to help make your soil a happy place for plants to grow!

YOU WILL NEED:

wooden crates/old fencing

fruit and vegetable scraps

grass cuttings

green leaves

brown leaves

newspapers

a watering can

soil

a shovel

HAPPY APPLE CRUMBLE

Apple crumble is a delicious treat after a windy walk. If you come home with some wild blackberries to add to it, it's even tastier. You can eat it warm from the oven with ice cream or cold the next day. Either way, it will make you and your friends very happy!

FOR THE FILLING, YOU WILL NEED:

1 pound apples (Granny Smith or Honeycrisp are best, but any kind works!)

3 ounces blackberries

2 tablespoons brown sugar

1 tablespoon lemon juice

1 teaspoon ground cinnamon

whipped cream or a small scoop vanilla ice cream (optional)

FOR THE CRUMBLE, YOU WILL NEED:

½ cup unsalted butter, softened

½ cup brown sugar

¾ cup flour

½ cup oats

TOTAL

**1 hour,
15 minutes**

**Makes 4–6
servings**

Ask a grown-up to preheat the oven to 325°F (160°C).

With a grown-up's help, peel the apples. You can also leave the skin on if you prefer—it's up to you! Then ask a grown-up to slice the apples and remove the cores.

For the filling, place the apple slices in an even layer in a baking dish. Add the berries on top, then sprinkle with sugar, lemon juice, and ground cinnamon.

For the crumble, combine the butter, sugar, flour, and oats together in a small bowl with your fingers to make a fine, crumbly mixture.

Sprinkle the crumble mixture over the fruit and ask a grown-up to put it on the middle shelf of the oven. Bake for 40–45 minutes, until the apples are soft when poked with a fork.

Allow the crumble to cool slightly before serving, as it will be very hot. Adding whipped cream or ice cream will help it cool faster and make it taste extra delicious!

NATURE MEMORY JAR

On your next vacation or family outing, try collecting special treasures to remind you of your adventure. It's a wonderful way of making memories last!

Decide what you want to highlight in your jar: the woods, the beach, your backyard, or any memory from your latest trip!

After you collect your nature treasures, leave them to dry completely, then place them carefully inside your jar. If you are creating a scene, you could put in a small layer of pea gravel first, which helps to hold everything in place. Or just toss it all in together in one happy mix!

Decorate the lid by gluing on more nature treasures. When the glue is dry, put the lid on the jar.

Write down where you went and when on a small piece of paper. Stick the paper on the front or bottom of your jar, or even slip it inside.

Keep your jar on a table or shelf so that every time you look at it, you'll remember the fun adventures you had!

You can make your jar into a nightlight by adding a string of solar or battery-powered LED lights. Sweet dreams!

TASTY GRANOLA

It's so much fun to toast your own granola. It's easy to make in big batches and it keeps for a few weeks in an airtight container. Add different types of nuts and dried fruits until you find your favorite mix.

Ask a grown-up to preheat the oven to 325°F (160°C).

Mix the oats, coconut, nuts, and seeds in a large bowl.

In a smaller bowl, mix together the syrup, sugar, oil, juice, vanilla, cinnamon, and salt.

Pour the wet mixture over the oat mixture and stir together so everything is nice and sticky all over, then spread it out evenly on a baking pan.

YOU WILL NEED:

5 cups whole oats

¾ cup shredded coconut

1 cup nuts, chopped or finely sliced: almonds, pecans, cashews, walnuts, hazelnuts, peanuts—or a mix

½ cup sunflower seeds or pumpkin seeds—or a mix

2 tablespoons maple syrup

2 tablespoons light brown sugar

⅓ cup sunflower or vegetable oil

½ cup apple juice

1 teaspoon vanilla extract

1 teaspoon ground cinnamon

1 teaspoon salt (optional)

1 cup dried fruit: raisins, chopped apricots, cranberries, blueberries, mango, pineapple—or a mix

Ask a grown-up to put your pans in the oven and let the granola bake for 20 minutes. Next, remove the granola from the oven and add the dried fruit, stirring well with a wooden spoon.

Ask a grown-up to put the pans back in the oven for another 10 minutes. But keep an eye on the granola to make sure it doesn't burn.

Once your granola is ready, ask a grown-up to take it out of the oven. Let it cool, then enjoy it with yogurt or milk!

CARVE A SPOOKY PUMPKIN

Halloween originates from an ancient Celtic festival, where people believed spirits could interact with them only on the last day of October. People wore costumes to confuse the ghosts and made lanterns to put by their doors.

Choose a plump pumpkin from your garden or a pumpkin patch. To make it last as long as possible, wait to carve it until just before Halloween. It helps to first draw a face on your pumpkin using a marker. It can be scary, funny, or both! Make sure to keep the eyes, nose, and mouth far apart.

Ask a grown-up helper to cut out the top of the pumpkin, carving in a circle around the stem to make a little hat.

Using a spoon, scrape out all the squishy insides. Now ask a grown-up to help you cut out the eyes, nose, and mouth. You can even make ears, if you like! Wipe off any extra marker marks with a damp paper towel.

Put your smiling pumpkin head where everyone can admire it, either inside your front window or outside on the front step. Place an LED light or lit tea light inside, pop the hat back on top, and stand back to admire your spooky pumpkin!

For extra Halloween fun, try decorating minipumpkins or squash by drawing faces on them with dark permanent markers!

YOU WILL NEED:

washable markers

a large carving knife

a large metal spoon

paper towel

a tea light or LED light

permanent markers (optional)

CRISPY CINNAMON STARS

Light up a dark fall afternoon with comforting cinnamon French toast! This sweet treat is fun to make and eat together with family or friends.

TOTAL

15 minutes

Makes
4 servings

Put the egg, milk, cinnamon, vanilla extract, and salt in a bowl, and beat it together using a fork.

Lay your slices of bread flat on a cutting board. Using a cookie cutter, carefully cut out star shapes from each slice. If you have a small cookie cutter, you might even be able to make more than one star from each piece of bread.

Soak your stars in the egg mixture until they are completely covered.

Now ask a grown-up to heat a lightly buttered frying pan over medium heat. When the pan is hot, ask a grown-up to carefully place the battered stars into the pan. Cook evenly on both sides, until the stars are crisp and lightly browned.

Sprinkle with cinnamon and serve warm as a super sparkly snack!

YOU WILL NEED:

1 egg

1/3 cup milk

1 tablespoon ground cinnamon

1 teaspoon vanilla extract

1 pinch salt

4 slices of bread

a star cookie cutter

CHALK DESIGNS

Chalk designs are a great way to decorate and create a friendly outdoor space. Find inspiration from and celebrate the Hindu festival of Diwali, where people make colorful rangoli patterns on the floor using natural materials.

Take a piece of chalk and draw an outline of your pattern on the sidewalk or driveway; always remember to ask for permission first.

Fill in the outlines with whatever you like. You can use brightly colored flower petals, leaves, or colored sand, or even uncooked rice, dried beans and lentils, spices, or grass.

If you are using sand, rice, or spices, use a paper cup to sprinkle them on the ground. Then try using a fork or spoon to make fine lines or patterns.

Finally, add some LED or battery-operated tea lights to really show off your design!

YOU WILL NEED:

colored chalk

flowers, leaves, or grass (dried or fresh)

colored sand

dry, uncooked rice

colorful dried beans and lentils

nonflammable spices, such as turmeric or nutmeg

small paper cups

a fork, spoon, or whisk

tea lights (LED or battery operated)

FANTASTIC BIRD FEAST

A fun, easy way to bring birds to your yard or balcony is to make a bird feeder—especially in fall and winter when it's harder to find food.

YOU WILL NEED:

a large
pine cone

two pieces of string,
each about 20 inches
(50 centimeters) long

a spoon

birdseed

peanut
butter

Fold the first piece of string in half.

Wrap the ends around the width of the pine cone (not too close to the top) and tie them into a double knot.

This will be the loop for hanging up your bird feeder.

Use a spoon (or your hands, if your pine cone isn't too prickly!) to smear peanut butter all over the pine cone, until it is thickly coated.

Sprinkle a handful of birdseed onto a plate or flat surface. Roll the pine cone in the birdseed until it is completely covered.

Fold the second piece of string in half, then thread it through the loop that you previously tied to your pine cone.

Tie the ends of the new loop together around a sturdy branch, wrapping it around a couple of times before tying a tight double knot.

Now go back inside and wait for the birds to come and nibble this tasty treat! Who will turn up today?

WINTER

Winter is wonderful! Even though many trees and plants look dead in the winter, they are really just sleeping. Like bears and other animals, plants hibernate too, resting until spring. There is so much fun to be had, indoors and out, whatever the winter weather brings!

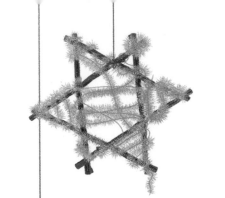

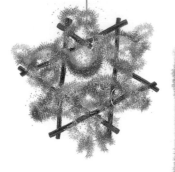

SHINING STARS

Sparkly stars are the perfect way to brighten your home during the dark winter months. You can hang these stars on a tree, a mantelpiece, or anywhere you like!

YOU WILL NEED:

5 or 6 smooth, straight twigs for each star

craft glue

twine, cut into about 12 small pieces per star, each 4–6 inches (12–15 centimeters) long

silver or gold paint (optional)

shiny ribbon or tinsel (optional)

SIX-POINTED STAR

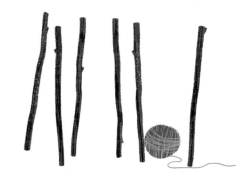

FIVE-POINTED STAR

Make sure your twigs are all about the same length. You may need a grown-up to help you cut them down.

Start with two twigs and make an upside-down V shape, with the tops overlapping a bit.

If you are making a six-pointed star, lay a third twig across the bottom of the V-shaped twigs to make a triangle. Use three twigs to make another triangle just like the first, then turn it upside down and lay it on top of the first triangle.

If you are making a five-pointed star, lay a third twig across the middle, about a third of the way down from the top, like a letter A. Use the fourth and fifth twigs to connect each of the long arms of the third twig to the ends of the upside-down V.

Now glue the twigs together carefully in every place where they cross over each other. All the ends should overlap a bit, which will make it easier to tie—and it will look better too! Let your star dry completely.

Wrap and tie a knot with twine at each point that the twigs cross, and cut off any loose ends. Now it's time to decorate! Try using shiny ribbons, tinsel, string, and paint to decorate your star however you like. You could even wrap fairy lights around your star to make it really shine!

FABULOUS FRUITY WRAPPING PAPER

All the nature art and crafts you have made so far make perfect presents, so here's a wonderful way to wrap them!

YOU WILL NEED:

some firm fruit and vegetables, such as apples, pears, or potatoes

a sharp knife (for grown-ups only!)

a cutting board

protective plastic covering (optional)

rolls of brown or white craft paper

water-based paint

plates or shallow bowls

Ask a grown-up to cut the fruit in half. Apples and unripe pears work best, as soft fruit makes the paint too watery.

Lay out a plastic covering or extra paper to catch any spills. Then, roll out your paper. Pour different colored paint into plates or bowls for easy dipping.

Dip the fruit into the paint, cut side down. If needed, dab any excess paint on a paper towel. Then stamp the fruit gently all over the paper to make a pretty pattern.

Once the paint is dry, wrap your presents. Surprise your friends and family with one of your beautiful creations— this showstopping paper will be part of the gift!

POTATO PRINTS

You can also try using a firm vegetable, such as a potato! Before you dip your potato into the paint, use a toothpick to poke patterns or shapes into the cut side of the potato, or ask a grown-up to cut your potato into different shapes, such as a star, to make your prints extra special!

CRAFTY HOLIDAY COOKIES

Get your paintbrushes ready, because these delicious cookies are part cooking, part craft project! And these treats are not just for the holiday season—you can make them anytime, in any shape you like! You'll want to start this project early in the morning, to allow time to chill the dough, decorate your cookies, and then taste a few!

YOU WILL NEED:

1 cup butter

1 cup granulated white sugar

2 eggs

1 teaspoon vanilla extract

2⅓ cups sifted flour

½ teaspoon salt

festive cookie cutters

In a big bowl, use an electric hand mixer to cream the butter until smooth. Then slowly add the sugar to the butter until it's light and fluffy. Now add the eggs one at a time to the sugar mixture, beating until smooth after each egg. Add the vanilla extract, then slowly and carefully add the flour and salt to the sugar mixture a little at a time. Mix well.

Cover the dough and refrigerate for two hours.

After the dough's chilled, preheat the oven to 375°F (190°C).

Sprinkle your work surface with a little flour and rub some flour on the rolling pin as well. Roll out the dough until it's about 1/8 inch thick. Sprinkle flour onto the cookie cutters to keep the dough from sticking—it might start to look like it's snowing in your kitchen! Now cut out shapes and lay them carefully on a baking sheet.

Bake for 12–15 minutes, watching carefully to make sure the cookies don't burn. Cool them completely on a wire rack, then get ready to decorate!

YOU WILL NEED:

2½ teaspoons light corn syrup

¾ teaspoon vanilla extract

4 tablespoons water

3 cups powdered sugar

food coloring

clean, new craft paintbrushes

Whisk the powdered sugar, vanilla, corn syrup, and water in a bowl until smooth. Add an extra teaspoon of water if icing is too thick.

Divide the icing into several containers (teacups or mugs are perfect). Add the desired food coloring to each container and stir well.

Now paint your cookies and leave them to dry. You can store them in a sealed container for up to a week and they make the perfect present for family and friends!

PRESENT IN A POT

Everyone loves a pretty plant, especially when it's in a pretty pot too! These early flowering bulbs make the perfect gift to brighten up the winter.

YOU WILL NEED:

amaryllis bulbs (these can make some animals very sick if they eat them, so be careful to keep them away from your pets)

plant pots, an inch or a few centimeters wider than the bulbs

acrylic paint

paintbrushes

permanent markers

ribbon

potting soil

Amaryllis bulbs normally grow in the spring, but you can make them think it's time to start growing by keeping them inside where it's warm!

Make sure to plant the bulbs six weeks before you plan to give them as a gift, to allow them enough time to grow.

Before you plant the bulbs, decorate the pot. Use acrylic paint or markers to draw a fun pattern or a picture on the pot. Or paint the pot a cheerful color and tie a ribbon around it in a pretty bow.

Once you've finished decorating the pot and the paint has dried completely, it's time to plant the bulbs.

First, fill the pot halfway with potting soil. Place the bulb pointy end up in the soil. Then carefully fill the pot with soil around the bulb, until only the top third of the bulb is uncovered. Press the soil firmly down around the bulb. Water well, and then keep the pot in a warm, dark place.

Leave the pot this way for about two weeks, until you see the tip of the first green shoot. At this point, move the pot to a warm, bright place. Start to water it again, just enough to keep the soil moist—be careful not to make the bulb too wet.

Watch the green shoots grow and make buds. Give them to your friends and family just as they're ready to burst into beautiful flowers!

WINTER WILDLIFE TREE

Rabbits, squirrels, and other wildlife don't have much to eat in winter when the trees and bushes are bare. Help these hungry animals by decorating an outdoor tree full of tasty treats for them to eat. You can make winter wildlife's wishes come true!

Ask a grown-up to heat the oil over medium-high heat in a large saucepan.
Drop the popcorn kernels in and put the lid on.
Turn up the heat and wait for the kernels to start popping.

Keep shaking the pan to prevent the popcorn from burning. As soon as the popping has slowed to 2–3 seconds between pops, the popcorn is ready. Remove from the heat, pour into a bowl, and wait until it cools.

When the popcorn has cooled completely, thread the needle with the string, and pull it through each kernel, alternating popcorn and cranberries—or making any pattern you like.

Once finished, take the garland outdoors and wrap it around a tree. You could even lay it over bushes or shrubs, or wrap it around the railing of a balcony. Now sit back and watch the winter wildlife have a very happy winter treat.

YOU WILL NEED:

3 tablespoons sunflower, coconut, or other vegetable oil

½ cup popcorn kernels

2 bags whole cranberries (about 24 ounces)

a large craft needle

thick string or knitting wool, about 10 feet (3 meters)

85

PERFECT POMANDERS

It's so much fun to turn an orange into a sweet-smelling pomander! You can hang one in a closet or room to make the air smell amazing. They also make great presents, especially during the festive season.

YOU WILL NEED:

some ribbon

1 orange

1 toothpick

1 small jar of dried whole cloves

First, carefully use a toothpick to poke a hole in the orange rind. Then poke a clove into the hole, using the pointy end. Do this until the whole orange is covered in cloves! Try creating different patterns or designs like a smiley face.

Lay out two strips of ribbon in an X shape. Place an orange in the center where the ribbons overlap. Lift the ribbons around the orange and tie them together in a bow.

When you're finished, hang the orange in a warm, airy place to dry out. After about four weeks, it should be completely dry. If it has shrunk a little bit, you might need to retie the ribbon a little tighter.

Now your pomander is ready to give to a lucky person, who will think of you every time they smell its lovely scent.

string, yarn, a scarf, or fabric—any color or thickness and lots of it!

a friendly tree (ask permission first if it's not in your own yard)

CHEERFUL TREE SWEATER

Some winter trees can look very bare without their leaves, flowers, and fruit. Try brightening one up with a colorful tree sweater!

If you know how to braid, you can start by braiding together different colors of yarn, but using a single strand works too! You can mix and match your materials however you like.

Loop your yarn, scarf, or fabric once around the tree's trunk and tie the end in a good, strong knot. Or run around the tree as quickly as you can, winding the yarn around the trunk again and again! Don't pull it too tight, so the tree can stretch and grow.

Wrap it high, wrap it low, and change the colors as you go— now the tree will be colorful and cozy! Remember to remove the sweater as spring arrives to allow new leaves and flowers the room to grow.

PLANT A TREE

Trees are home to birds, squirrels, butterflies, and other wildlife. They make oxygen, which is what we breathe in. Trees help keep us healthy.

The best time to plant trees is late fall or the early winter months, as long as the ground is not too frozen. Make sure to choose the right kind of tree for your space: it needs room to grow.

YOU WILL NEED:

a large empty patch of soil

a sapling (a baby tree)

a shovel

mulch

Dig a hole three times as wide as the ball of roots at the bottom of the sapling.

Place the tree inside the hole, keeping the trunk straight, then fill the hole back in with soil.

Put a layer of mulch around the tree to keep water in and weeds away. Watch that the layer isn't too thick—it should be no more than an inch or so.

HERE ARE A FEW TYPES OF TREES
TO PLANT TO HELP THE EARTH:

spruce

apple

holly

beech

COZY CHICKEN PIE

Pies are the perfect dinner treat for cold evenings. This recipe makes one big pie for four to six people. Serve with buttery peas for a delicious meal!

TOTAL

1 hour (or 1 hour, 20 minutes if making pastry; see page 44 for a recipe)

Makes 4–6 servings

see page 44 for a recipe

YOU WILL NEED:

shortcrust pastry (doubled; see page 44 for recipe) or two 14-ounce pie shells

4 chicken breasts, cut into 1-inch chunks

½ cup unsalted butter

¾ cup flour

1 cup milk

⅔ cup heavy cream

1 cup low-sodium chicken stock

1 teaspoon salt (optional)

1 egg, beaten

Ask a grown-up to preheat the oven to 350°F (180°C).

Divide your pastry into two even balls or start with one premade pastry dough. Then, using plenty of flour on your rolling pin and work space, roll the pastry out to about ¼ inch (5 millimeters) thick and slightly larger than the pie dish.

Line the pie dish with one of the pastry circles and prick with a fork in several places. Cut off any overhanging pastry with a table knife. Put the chicken chunks into your pastry-lined dish. Then wash your hands and ask a grown-up to melt butter in a saucepan over low heat.

Add the flour to the melted butter and stir to make a smooth paste. Then slowly add the milk, heavy cream, stock, and salt. Bring to a boil, stirring nonstop until the mixture is thick and glossy and there are no lumps.

Ask a grown-up to pour the mixture over the chicken. Now you can cover your pie with the second pastry. Pinch the top and sides of the pie together with your thumbs—this will keep in all the yummy flavors!

Use a fork to prick a few holes in the top and then brush the top pastry with the beaten egg. Cook for 1 hour, or until the pie is golden brown.

TERRIFIC TERRARIUMS

When it's wet and cold outside, why not bring the garden inside?
These tiny gardens in jars and bowls are called terrariums. Will you make a
Jurassic jungle jumping with dinosaurs or a flowery, fern-filled fairyland?

YOU WILL NEED:

a very large, clean, dry
glass jar at least 8 inches
(20 centimeters) tall
or another clear glass
container such as a small
fish bowl

a few handfuls of
pea gravel

activated filtering
charcoal

potting soil

a teaspoon

a few small plants that
like plenty of moisture
and bright, indirect light
(see examples at the
bottom of the page)

a spray bottle of water

shells, twigs, or tiny toys

BEST PLANTS FOR TERRARIUMS:

Succulents might look super in an open terrarium, but
it can be really tricky to keep them happy and healthy,
so it's best for beginners to stick to this list—or use other
moisture-loving plants!

violas

miniature ivies

Before you start, wash and dry your jar or fish bowl well to make sure it is shiny and clean.

Put about 1 inch (2 centimeters) of pea gravel in the bottom of your jar or bowl. Add about 1 inch (2 centimeters) of activated charcoal on top. Then add 1–1½ inches (3–4 centimeters) of soil.

Use a teaspoon to dig a tiny hole in the soil and place your first plant carefully into it.

Gently press down the soil around your plant.

Continue planting until your jar or fish bowl is full, taking care to leave some space around each plant to let it grow.

When you are finished, spray the plants with water, but not too much. If you like, add some toy figures, shells, or twigs.

Place your terrific terrarium in bright (but not direct) sunlight and enjoy the wonderful world you've made!

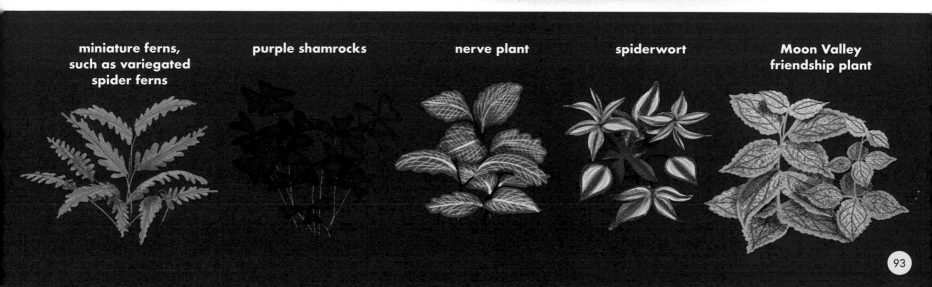

miniature ferns, such as variegated spider ferns

purple shamrocks

nerve plant

spiderwort

Moon Valley friendship plant

MAKE A PINE CONE PAL

Pine cones can be used to make all kinds of animals and friends. You could create a whole forest full of animals or make up your own magical creatures! Here are some ideas to get you started.

YOU WILL NEED:

scissors

colored paper or felt

glue

markers

googly eyes

clean, dry pine cones of different sizes

feathers or dried leaves

cotton balls

colored string

pipe cleaners

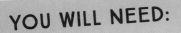

HEDGEHOG

Cut out a triangle from paper or felt, with slightly rounded points.

Either stick or draw a little nose onto one point, then glue googly eyes above it.

When the glue is dry, lay the pine cone on its side. Stick the triangle face just above the center of the pointy end of the pine cone, to make a perfectly prickly pine cone pet!

OWL

Cut out two small circles of paper or felt, and a small orange or yellow triangle. Glue googly eyes onto the circles.

When the glue is dry, sit the cone upright on its wide end and glue the eyes onto the upper half. Stick on the triangle, one tip pointing down, as a beak.

Add feathers, dried leaves, or paper or felt ovals to the sides of the cones for wings. Whoooo's a great artist? You are!

CAT

If you have a pine cone with big spaces between the scales, you don't need glue! Poke cotton balls into the spaces until the cone is completely covered in cotton.

Cut out two short pointy ears and a long tail from paper, string, or felt. Stand your pine cone up on its wide end and glue the ears and tail onto your cone. Add a pair of googly eyes to the front.

Twist two short pieces of pipe cleaner together to make an X shape, then glue these below the eyes to make cat whiskers!

GOOEY GRILLED CHEESE

When you've been out and about, a grilled cheese
is a quick and delicious lunch for a busy day!

TOTAL

10 minutes
Makes 1 sandwich

With a grown-up's help, slice or grate the cheese. Grated cheese melts faster, but keep your fingers away from the holes on the grater—you don't want a knuckle sandwich!

Ask a grown-up to heat the frying pan over low heat.

Butter one side of your slices of bread. Make sure to use enough butter so that the bread doesn't stick to the pan. Place the buttered side of one slice of bread facedown on a plate and sprinkle or lay the cheese and any extra fixings on the bread. Then add the second slice of bread buttered side faceup.

Ask a grown-up to slide your sandwich into the hot pan with a spatula. Let it cook it for 2–3 minutes on each side, turning as needed so it doesn't burn.

Remove from the heat, let it cool, then cut it into squares or triangles. Enjoy your grilled cheese and repeat the recipe for more!

YOU WILL NEED:

2 slices of bread

**¼ cup or 2 slices of cheese
(such as cheddar, Muenster,
or mozzarella)**

butter

**extra fixings (optional):
sliced ham, tomato,
pear, or apple**

PICTURE TREASURE HUNT

This activity makes nature walks even more fun. You will end up with a keepsake from your adventure that you can treasure forever!

Flip through magazines for pictures of animals and plants you might find on your outdoor adventure. Or, if you like to draw, then bring along a notebook and some colored pencils to draw them instead!

If you decide to collage, cut out the pictures you find and glue them onto the paper, leaving a little extra space around each one.

You can either make a sheet of nature pictures for everyone in your group or make one to do together as a team. When the glue is dry, write down the name of each animal and plant to help you keep track of them on your nature walk.

Bring your nature pages with you on your day out. See how many of the animals and plants you can find! Circle, check off, or cross out each one with your pen as you go—then, when you're done, take your completed pages home to keep as a reminder of your nature adventure!

YOU WILL NEED:

10–12 nature pictures from magazines or the internet

crayons, colored pencils, or markers

a blank notebook or printer paper

scissors

glue

a pen

TOOLS AND MATERIALS

CRAFT

- shells
- feathers
- leaves
- flowers
- pebbles
- twigs
- construction paper and card stock
- glue
- paint
- pine cones
- ribbons
- googly eyes
- colored pipe cleaners
- paintbrushes
- craft sticks
- cardboard (thin and thick—old boxes are ideal)
- scissors
- tape
- string
- twine
- ribbon
- hole punch
- felt
- smock (old T-shirts work well)

KITCHEN

- baking pans
- blender
- colander
- frying pan
- grater
- kitchen scissors
- knives (for grown-ups only!)
- ladle
- measuring spoons
- apron
- mixing bowls in different sizes
- cutting board
- pot holders
- vegetable peeler
- pie or quiche dish
- saucepans
- measuring cups
- sieve
- spatulas (a metal one for flipping and a softer one for scraping)
- a sturdy step stool (so little chefs can safely reach the countertop)
- wooden spoons
- tongs
- piping bag
- electric hand mixer
- rolling pin

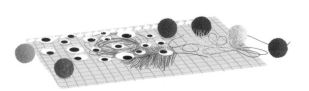

TOOLS AND MATERIALS

ADVENTURE

- hat
- sturdy shoes
- sunscreen
- water bottle
- light backpack
- snacks
- binocular
- magnifying glass
- rain jacket
- empty bag for garbage
- stopwatch
- notebook
- pen or pencil

GARDEN

- wooden plant markers or craft sticks
- rubber boots
- small watering can
- children's gardening gloves
- sun hat
- potting soil
- spray bottle
- small rake
- bucket
- shovel
- sand
- plant pots or containers

SAFETY TIPS

- It's important to be careful in the kitchen, especially when using sharp knives or a hot stove. Some parts of these recipes will need a grown-up to help peel and chop, or heat things up in a pan. Avoid wearing long sleeves in the kitchen so that they don't get caught in any food.

- Always wash your hands carefully before starting to cook, as well as between touching different kinds of ingredients. Keep raw meat—and any plates or utensils you've used for it—away from other ingredients, especially cooked food.

- Some garden tools can be sharp or very heavy, so grown-ups will need to help with these. It's a good idea to wear gardening gloves—every yard is different, and gloves will protect you from any hidden weeds that might irritate your skin.

- Wear sturdy shoes outdoors—you never know what might be slippery when you're out and about! Make sure a grown-up is always there when you're near rivers, ponds, or other bodies of water.

- Always be cautious if you aren't sure what a flower, leaf, or berry is—look it up when you are back at home and try to spot it on your next trip outside once you know that it is safe to touch or eat.

- Respect stinging insects; the outdoors is just as much their home as it is yours. Never hit or wave at wasps or bees—try to stay still and give them space until they fly away.

- Wear old clothes with long sleeves for messy art activities and wash them separately from your normal clothes. Always make sure that paints and powders are safe for the skin before touching them.

INDEX

baking 18–19, 44–45,
       64–65, 68–69, 82–83,
       90–91

beach 30–31, 40–41

bees 26, 34, 36–37, 50–51,
       102

bird feeders 74–77, 85

birds 51, 74–77, 85, 88

boats 40–41, 48

books 49

bottles 23, 38–39

branches 10–11, 12–13, 16,
       23, 55, 60–61, 74

bulbs 62, 84

cake 18–19

cardboard 22, 34–35

card stock 12–13, 42–43, 49

cheese 18–19, 28, 44–45,
       96–97

cinnamon 18–19, 64–65,
       68–69, 72

coconut 33, 68–69, 85

collages 12–13, 98

coloring 10, 12–13, 15,
       98–99

compost 34, 62–63

cooking 28, 32–33, 44–45,
       56–57, 64–65,
       68–69, 72, 82–83, 85,
       90–91, 96–97, 102

crafts 10–11, 12–13, 14–15,
       27, 42–43, 46–47, 49,
       54–55, 58–59, 66–67,
       70–71, 73, 78–79,
       80–81, 82–83, 86,
       94–95, 98–99

crayons 10–13, 15, 50, 98

crowns 27, 47

cutters 44–45, 72, 82–83

daisies 26–27, 49

daisy chains 27

dinner 28, 56–57, 90–91

drawing 15, 36, 42–43, 50,
       70–71, 73, 84, 94,
       98–99

dye 14–15

eggs 14–15, 18, 44–45, 72,
       82–83, 90–91

exercise 16–17, 60–61

fertilizer 34–35

fish bowls 92–93

flowers 10–13, 21, 26–27,
       29, 34, 36–37, 47, 49,
       54–55, 58–59, 62,
       66–67, 73, 84, 87,
       92–93, 102

flower pressing 49

fruit 20, 32–33, 63–65,
       68–69, 80–81, 85–87

gardening 20–22, 24–26, 29,
       34–35, 38–39, 51,
       62–63, 84, 88–89,
       92–93

glitter 14–15, 46, 62–63, 84,
       88–89, 92–93

glue 12–15, 22, 42–43,
       46–47, 58–59, 66–67,
       78–79, 94–95, 98–99

googly eyes 46, 94–95

granola 68–69

grass 22, 36, 63, 73

growing flowers 21, 26, 29,
       38–39, 51, 62, 84

growing fruit 20–21

growing vegetables 21, 29,
       34–35, 51

holiday 14–15, 18–19, 78–85

insects 26, 34, 36–37, 50–51,
       98–99, 102

instruments 23

jars 24–25, 66–67, 86, 92–93

leaf/leaves 7, 10–11, 12–13,
       25, 42–43, 47, 48–49,
       52, 54–55, 58–59,
       60–61, 63, 66–67, 73,
       87, 92–95, 102

leaf pressing 49

leaf rubbing 11

LED lights 66–67, 70–71, 73

meadows 26

memory jars 66–67

music 23

notebooks 36–37, 50–51

oats 64–65, 68–69

oil 18–19, 28, 56–57, 68–69, 72, 85, 96–97

oranges 86

paint 10, 12–14, 22, 42–43, 46, 79, 80–84, 91, 102

paper 22, 36–37, 47, 49, 62, 66–67, 73, 80–81, 94–95, 98–99

peas 21, 28, 29, 56–57, 90–91

planting 20–21, 24–25, 26, 29, 34–35, 38–39, 51, 62, 84, 88–89, 92–93

plants 16, 20–21, 24–25, 26–27, 29, 34–35, 36, 38–39, 50–51, 54, 62–63, 84, 87, 88–89, 92–93, 98

pine cones 55, 58–59, 74–75, 94–95

potato prints 81

preparing food 18–21, 28, 32–33, 44–45, 56–57, 64–65, 68–69, 72, 74–75, 82–83, 85, 90–91, 96–97, 102

pumpkin carving 70–71

pumpkins 21, 34–35, 68–71

presents 42–43, 46, 80–84, 86

rakes 26, 29, 62–63

raspberries 20, 32

recycling/reusing 23, 38–39, 63

rubber boots 38–39

safety tips 58, 102

sand 26, 40–41, 62, 73

sandcastles 40–41

saplings 88–89

seeds 10, 20, 22, 24–26, 29, 34–36, 54–55, 68–69, 74–75

shells 12–13, 14–15, 40–43, 58–59, 66–67, 92–93

shovels 26, 34–35, 38–39, 62, 88–89

smoothies 32

soil 20–22, 26, 29, 34–35, 38–39, 54–55, 62–63, 84, 88–89, 92–93

spray bottles 20, 22, 24–25, 92–93

stars 72, 78–79, 81

stretching 16–17, 61, 87

string 29, 47, 58–59, 78–79

tape 22–23

tea lights 70–71, 73

tomatoes 21, 56–57, 96–97

toys 22, 40–41, 92–93

twigs 10–11, 12–13, 23, 42–43, 48, 54–55, 58–61, 66–67, 78–79, 92–93

vegetables 18–19, 21, 24–25, 29, 34–35, 44–45, 51, 56–57, 63, 70, 81

watches 60–61

watering cans 26, 29, 34–35, 38–39, 62–63

wool 24–25, 47, 58–59, 74–75, 85, 87, 94–95

yoga 16–17